Comforting Little Hearts

Understanding Death

Balloons for Trevor

Written by Anne Good Cave
Illustrated by Janice Skivington

CPH
SAINT LOUIS

Comforting Little Hearts
Series Titles

Why Don't We Live Together Anymore? (Understanding Divorce)
When Will I Feel Better? (Understanding Chronic Illness)
I Have a New Family Now (Understanding Blended Families)
Balloons for Trevor (Understanding Death)

To Alex

Copyright © 1998 Anne Good Cave
Published by Concordia Publishing House
3558 S. Jefferson Avenue, St. Louis, MO 63118-3968
Manufactured in the United States of America

1   2   3   4   5   6   7   8   9   10   07   06   05   04   03   02   01   00   99   98

Trevor was my best buddy. He lived next door, and we played together every day. Sometimes we raced little cars. Sometimes we rode bikes. And sometimes we just climbed up on the doghouse and talked.

On his birthday I gave Trevor a racetrack and some cars. We set up the track all around his living room and raced our cars. I wasn't even mad when his car won!

On my birthday Trevor was sick and couldn't come to my party. I saved him some balloons and prizes and some cake and ice cream. We had our own party the next day, just the two of us.

One day I saw a fire engine and a police car at Trevor's house. I couldn't wait to go over and look at them, but Mom and Dad wouldn't let me.

Later that day Mom and Dad said they wanted to talk to me. Dad had a strange look on his face, and Mom was crying. We sat on the couch and Dad told me that Trevor had died during the night.

"Trevor had something wrong with his body and it quit working," Dad said.

"When is he coming back to life again?" I asked.

"Trevor won't come back to life again on earth," Dad explained. "God has given Trevor a new life in heaven."

I didn't know what to say. I was sure that this wasn't really happening. But why did Mom and Dad look so serious? And why did I feel so strange? I was cold inside and I shivered. Mom hugged me close.

Dad rubbed my back. "Trevor loved Jesus and believed that Jesus died on the cross for him," Dad continued. "When a person who loves Jesus dies, God takes that person to be with Him in heaven. Even though we don't have Trevor here to play with anymore, we can remember him. What is your favorite memory about Trevor?"

I thought for a minute. Then I remembered the time when we went camping at the beach. While Mom and Dad were putting up the tent, I looked around. I spotted Trevor right away. He and his parents were camping right next to us!

"Remember when Trevor was at the beach and we got to play together all weekend?" I smiled just remembering it.

I started to feel a little better, but something inside me was still sad and scared.

"Mom," I asked, "is my body going to quit working too?"

"Oh, honey," Mom said, pulling me up on her lap, "probably not. It is unusual for a child to die. Many people live to be very old. God has so much for you to do that He doesn't want you to worry about when you will die. If you get scared, just talk to me or Daddy about it."

For a few days, everything was different around our house. Mom cried a lot. I wasn't sad, but I wasn't happy either. I was nothing. It was like there was a big lump of ice inside me that wouldn't go away. It was there all the time, even at night.

Sometimes I woke up at night and wondered where Trevor was and what he was doing. Sometimes I was scared that I was going to die too.

"Mom?" I would call out. "When am I going to die?" Mom and Dad would let me crawl up in the middle of their big, warm bed.

"Sshhh," Mom would whisper. "Go ahead and cry, honey. Everything's going to be all right."

I would bury my face in Mom's soft nightgown and let the tears come out. It made my eyes all hot and my throat sore. But I felt better somehow.

One day I saw lots of people coming and going at Trevor's house. Mom told me that there was going to be a special church service, called a funeral, for Trevor. Trevor's body would be placed in a special box. After the service everyone would go to a place called a cemetery where the box would be put into the ground.

"You see, Trevor's body stayed after he died," Mom said. "It's like when you take off your clothes and leave them on the floor. Jesus will fix Trevor's body for his new life in heaven. Do you think you want to come to the funeral with us? It's important to say good-bye to Trevor."

I thought about it and thought about it. I wanted to be with Mom and Dad, but I didn't think I wanted to go to the funeral. I didn't like seeing Trevor's mom and dad crying all the time. I didn't think I wanted to see the box with Trevor's body in it. I *knew* I didn't want to see the cemetery. I'd heard about cemeteries. Weren't they those spooky places you heard about at Halloween?

So Grandma came to stay with me while Mom and Dad went to Trevor's funeral and to the cemetery. When they came home, they hugged me and held me tight. I still had that lump of ice inside me. Every day I hoped the ice would melt, but it didn't. I felt angry all the time, but I didn't know whom to be angry at.

Peter came over. He was Trevor's friend too, but he'd never played with me much. I guessed with Trevor gone we'd have to play together. Peter told me that Trevor died because he was such a good boy that God wanted him to live in heaven. That scared me.

I ran out into the street. Mom called to me to get back on the sidewalk, but I wouldn't. I wanted to make her angry too.

"I don't know what's gotten into you," Mom said.

"I don't want to be a good boy! I don't want God to make me die!" I shouted. Didn't Mom and Dad understand anything?

I went over to Peter's house to play.

"Do you want to go see Trevor?"
Peter asked me.

"Yes!" I was excited. "How?"

"All you have to do is die. Then you'll go to heaven and see Trevor."

I wasn't so sure about that. I wished Trevor would come down from heaven and visit me. I told my mom about it that night.

Mom hugged me tight. "We can't go visit Trevor in heaven, honey," she said. "Only God knows when it is time for us to be born or to die. And it doesn't have anything to do with whether we are good or bad. Jesus died to take the punishment for the bad things we do. We will probably die when we are very old. Then we will live in heaven with Jesus, just like Trevor."

The next day my mom went to visit Peter's mom. She came home all excited. "Honey, I found out about a special group," Mom told me. "It's for kids who are sad because someone they love has died. They can talk to one another about how they feel. Would you like to try it?"

At first I didn't want to go. But since Peter was going, I decided I would too. At the first meeting we talked about the person we loved who had died. I told the other kids about Trevor, how we had raced cars and played video games together.

I missed Trevor so much it hurt to talk about him. The other kids were hurting too. One girl's father had died. Another boy's brother had died. I was sad for them, but I felt a little warmer inside, like the ice was starting to melt just a little bit.

The next week, we talked about our feelings. I was sad that Trevor had died, but I was angry too. How could Trevor die? He was my best friend. Now I didn't have a best friend to play with anymore. I didn't want to be buddies with anyone but Trevor.

Then I felt guilty because I shouldn't be angry. It wasn't Trevor's fault that he died. And what about the other kids in the group? Some of them had lost part of their family. That must feel even worse than having your best friend die.

Then I felt embarrassed because I was so angry and sad and scared all at once. I didn't know what I was feeling sometimes. I was so confused that I didn't even want to talk about it.

One day Mom took me to the cemetery. It wasn't spooky or scary at all! It was like a park with lots of green grass and big trees. There were lots of stones with the names carved on them of the people who had died.

We found Trevor's gravestone. There were toys placed all around it. I had brought along a basket of things that reminded me of Trevor. Inside it I'd put the race car he always played with at my house, a pretty rock, a feather I found in my backyard, a pinwheel that spun when the wind blew, and a picture of me.

Mom laid a big piece of paper on the stone and we rubbed crayons over the paper until the words came through:

Trevor William McIntosh
We Will Always Love You.

I felt hot tears in my eyes as we colored, and I looked up to see Mom crying too. I hardly noticed that the ice inside me had melted just a little bit more.

Peter and I kept going to our grief group. On the last day we drew a picture of the way things used to be. My picture showed Trevor and me playing video games. Then we drew a picture of the way things are now. I drew our van at the cemetery, when we visited Trevor's grave.

The counselor gave me a little sack filled with some pretty rocks. Some of the rocks were smooth and polished, and others were rough and sharp. She said that my feelings are like the rocks—some are smooth and nice, and some are rough and sharp.

I held the rocks in my hand. At first they were cold, but soon they got warm from being held. I remembered when it felt as if my tummy was full of cold, hard ice. Now the ice was so small, I hardly ever noticed it. Did this mean I would forget Trevor?

Today was Trevor's birthday. I remembered that just a year ago we had played together, laughing and racing cars.

Mom and Dad and I took some kids to plant a tree for Trevor at the park. We put a stone under the tree, just like the gravestone, to help people remember Trevor. The sun was shining, but I felt cold inside. The piece of ice is very tiny, but I still notice it sometimes.

Dad gave each of us a glow-in-the-dark star to put on our bedroom ceilings. That's so when we go to bed at night, we can look up and remember that Trevor is in heaven. I'm going to say good-night to Trevor every night.

After we planted the tree, Peter's mom gave everyone a balloon. We sang "Happy Birthday" to Trevor. I held my mom's hand and reached for Dad's. When I realized I had let go of my balloon, it was too late. I looked up and watched the balloon float up into that bright blue sky toward heaven. I wondered if Trevor had a balloon in heaven. Well, he does now.

A Note to Parents

If someone your child knows has died, keep in mind that the grief he or she feels is very real. Your child does understand what is happening, even if he or she doesn't show grief in a way you would expect.

Do be honest with your child. Avoid such euphemisms as "He's gone away." "The good die young." "She has passed on." "He's sleeping with the angels now." Because children think in concrete terms, these phrases can be confusing and frightening. **Don't avoid the subject of death.** Bring it up gently and try to encourage your child to talk to you.

Do permit your child to cry. Crying is a healthy release. Don't ask your child to "be brave" or "take it like a man (or woman)."

Do accept whatever feelings your child may be having. Remember, children's feelings often change quickly. Try to help your child label his or her feelings: "You feel scared." "You feel guilty." "You are angry."

Do give your child the opportunity to remember his or her loved one. Planting a special tree, creating a collage, or putting together a scrapbook are just a few positive activities.

Do ask your pastor, funeral director, or a counselor for advice and resources. Often experts recommend that a grieving child attend the funeral, if it will not be a frightening experience, so the child will experience some closure. These individuals can offer appropriate advice for your situation.